Acknowledgements

To my husband, Bill...love, friend and companion, who helps me be me.

Also to Sandy Shaffer, Dottie Ross, (..and, of course, dear, creative Rosemary Kordowski) teachers and friends whose advice and editing help were invaluable. Thank you all.

CONTENTS

INTRODUCTION

1. GO FORTH AND TEACH!......................1
Adult Education: "Winging" it in the Olden Days

2. ADAPT, ADAPT ADAPT!
Men's Room Available...Suitable for Class.....5
Making the Best of a Bad Situation

3. ADULTS ARE NOT CHILDREN
NO KIDDING!...................................... 10
Respecting Your Students as Adults

4. DESIGN FOR SUCCESS.....................12
Creating a Climate for Adult Learning

5. LEARNING WITH STYLE.....................14
Discover Your Student's Unique Learning Style,
And Use It to Its Best Advantage

6. MAKE THE MOST OF YOUR
APPROACH SHOT!...............................17
Easing up to Your "Fragile Learners" at That First Encounter

NO KIDDING!

A PRIMER FOR TEACHERS OR TUTORS NEW TO ADULT EDUCATION

Jane Hallock Combs

LONGMUIR/JONES PUBLISHING COMPANY
LARGO, FLORIDA

Longmuir/Jones Publishing Company
11014-117th Way N., Suite E
Largo, FL. 34648
813-398-4090

Artwork by Norma J. Lewis
Printed and bound in the United States of America
ISBN 0-9625440-0-0

7. LET'S GET GOING.................................22
Getting Your Students Started on a "Winning" Track

8. CANDY, FLOWERS, AND PICKLED
OCTOPUS!.................................24
Perks of the Profession?

9. TYPES OF ADULT LEARNERS..................26
Older Adults, Adults in Nursing Homes, Immigrants,
the Handicapped, Displaced Homemakers, the
Institutionalized, Adults in Rural and Urban Centers

10. THOSE *LOVELY* VOLUNTEERS...
GOD BLESS THEM!.................................36
Selection and Use of a Great Resource

11. CHARACTERISTICS OF ADULT
LEARNERS.................................40
Adults of All Sizes, Shapes and Psyches

12. RULES TO REMEMBER.................................44

13. NOW FORWARD!.................................45
Challenge and Opportunity Await!

APPENDIX

INTRODUCTION

So you've been teaching school for eighteen years...or eighty...or eight months. You KNOW about teaching! But you've just taken on a new assignment. Instead of elementary aged kids, high schoolers, or...ye gods!...middle schoolers, you've opted to pick up an evening class or two in adult education. Or perhaps you've decided to switch fields altogether and move full time into adult ed away from your comfortable, familiar classroom. OR you're a tutor about to step into your first adult ed tutorial role. Great! This book is for all of you.

The adult education field is burgeoning these days, and more and more teachers and tutors (neophytes and old-hands alike) are finding themselves in classrooms filled with adults. It's a new experience, but an exciting one. This book is designed to help you better understand this new world into which you are stepping. Good luck! Hold on to your hats and ENJOY!

1. GO FORTH AND TEACH!

In the olden days, like 1971, when adult education was getting geared up...a new teacher (if lucky) had a brief interview with whoever was adult education director in that particular city or county. (You might even have had a quickie interview with whatever principal to whom you might be reporting.) Then you were told the location of your class, what time it met...and...given a hearty handshake... sent off to do your thing sans orientation, sans understanding of what was expected of you, and sans any sort of materials.

Breathes there a teacher with soul so dead who can't go out there and wing it before a group of adult strangers sitting uncomfortably in third grade seats? Sure! Lots of us will panic when faced with a crowd of adults expecting to learn "God knows what" especially if we feel ill prepared to teach them. There's something about all those expectant faces..............and that empty feeling in the pit of your stomach... and that wild desire to RUN!

I remember my first evening when I went forth to teach

E.S.L.* to a group of gentlemen in Rochester, N.Y.

The class was to be held in a room in The Puerto Rican Club somewhere in downtown Rochester. My sole qualifications for the job were that I had taught (for one year...high school English) and that I knew some Spanish (enough to get me to ladies' rooms around Central America, but not much more. I assumed they had a ladies' room in the Puerto Rican Club . That would help).

It was a snowy, wet night in Rochester (like most nights there.) I walked into the club armed with the single copy of Dixon's "English Step By Step With Pictures" I had weedled out of the adult ed director and class plans that I figured should have gotten me through the allotted three hours and then some. I figured wrong. Fifteen minutes later, I had gone through everything I had planned. The gentlemen were smiling, but beyond the smiles lurked perplexed expressions and a tinge of sadness.

They had smiled and nodded and been so agreeable everytime I had asked them, "Do you understand?", that I hadn't realized they didn't have the foggiest notion of what in the world I was talking about.

I went to the ladies' room.

....

* English as a Second Language

RULE #1: WHEN WORKING WITH ADULTS, ASSUME NOTHING!

I'd thought of spending the night in the ladies' room, but it was cramped and dark and I'd eventually have to come out. I was certain that when I did, those eager, pleasant faces would still be there waiting for me because "the teacher" had not said they could go. (One of the best things about working with adults...especially foreign adults... is that they are SO COURTEOUS!)

Coward I may be, but teacher I am. I came out of the ladies' room at last, then went back to the beginning of "English Step by Step" and started over. This time I paid less attention to those smiles and   nodding heads. (For that matter, I didn't pay much attention to the book either. We needed basics.)

"I am a teacher." I pounded my chest á la *Tarzan'*.
"You are students." I pointed to them.

I finally got them up to introducing themselves.

"Hi! My name is Jane. I'm a teacher." I would intone.

"Hi!   My name is Roberto, I'm a student," Roberto would come back at me.

By the end of the evening, everyone was introducing himself to everyone else . It was going well except for Paco who never did get the hang of it and dropped out of class before too long. As far as I know to this day he is wandering around somewhere in Rochester occasionally bursting into the only English he knows:

"Hi! My name is Jane. I'm a teacher!"

2. ADAPT, ADAPT, ADAPT!

Men's room available...suitable for class

All teachers must be flexible, (it goes with the territory), but teachers of adult education must be more flexible than a rubber band and more adaptable than a chameleon. You never know what's going to happen next...or where! You must be ready to adapt or die trying! (Well dying's going a bit far, but you get the drift.)

In K-12 one is *usually* assured of a place to rest one's head (or other parts of one's anatomy). A classroom is something of a given. Not so in adult ed.

Plato, the first well-known adult educator, started out under a tree. Many of us have not been that lucky. One of my friends, Mary Anne, who is more flexible than a Czech gymnast, recently began a teaching stint (ABE/GED)* in the local YWCA. A refugee from a middle school, she was thrilled by the prospect   of her first adult ed assignment. She was less than thrilled when she saw her classroom.

The walls were dark with mildew (mingled nicely with dirt). There was, of course, no chalkboard. (Veteran adult ed teachers always carry portable chalkboards in the trunks of their cars). The tables which were to serve as desks for the students were more scarred and traumatized than super bowl losers.

Mary Anne eventually was able to paint the walls, and she brightened things up a lot with hanging baskets of colorful silk flowers. The tables she covered with cheerful contact paper, and from   somewhere she confiscated an   old, war - weary   but useable swivel topped chalkboard. Her main problem with the room was not so easy to fix.

Her classroom was partitioned off by folding doors from two other rooms one of which contained an aerobics exercise class while the other housed the local drum corps on alternate Tuesdays. Between days when the drum corps met, another aerobics class was held. This one was "Low Impact Aerobics." The impact may have been low; the music wasn't.

"THIS IS OUR CHALLENGE," Mary Anne would chortle...loudly. "THINK YOU ARE AT HOME. Those are   YOUR children in the next room. We DO NOT HEAR THEM!" She would shout.

....

* Adult Basic Education/General Educational Development

Some of Mary Anne's shouting got through to the aerobics classes. They're not as loud as they used to be...or maybe they simply don't bother people as much. You can get used to anything.   As Mary Anne would say, "Put enough flowers around and smile a lot and soon that's all anyone will notice!" It works well for her!

RULE 2: BRIGHTEN THE CORNER WHERE YOU ARE ... EVEN IF IT IS A BUSY INTERSECTION!

During my nineteen years in adult education, I have taught in tiny rooms no bigger than a closet (equipped with folding metal chairs, no desks). I've taught in busy cafeterias where people intent on food would only stop banging and rattling their trays long enough to come over and kibitz the teacher. I've taught in long, narrow halls and out under trees by a sparkling lake. I 've taught in a roach-infested girl's club where the bugs outnumbered the students thirty to one, but one of the most interesting "classrooms" I have ever seen was one that had for its location the men's room of a crowded adult center! Actually, it was a classroom fashioned out of what had been the vestibule of the men's room. It had been a place where the male students had lounged   and   talked   and   smoked   an occasional cigarette...LOTS of occasional cigarettes! When Fran Tibbetts finished with it, it was all classroom.

Fran had been sharing a huge room with four other

teachers. A room which doubled as an auditorium in our large adult center, it could hold more than the seventy + souls we had in there (including space for portable chalkboards, file cabinets, etc.) but the classes were in English as a second language which are nothing if not vocal. Five vocal classes going on at the same time created a cacophoney which even Fran, a survivor, could not handle. She went to the principal and pleaded for a place of her own.

When he jokingly said the only spare place was the anteroom to the men's room on the 2nd floor, she said:

"Fine! I"ll take it!"

Before he could splutter that he'd only been kidding, Fran was long gone. She had rounded up the custodian, gathered tables, chairs, movable partitions, posters and a chalkboard. Fran had everything set up before anyone knew what had happened.

There were a lot of surprised faces going in and out of the men's room for a while, and Fran had to occasionally speak loudly to overcome the noise of running water. But she had her OWN room, and she radiated happiness. You might almost say Fran was flush with success!

****

<u>REMEMBER!</u>

1. If your room is not quite as you'd like it, *D O SOMETHING ABOUT IT!* Simple straightening up can do wonders. Adding posters, flowers or plants can give the room a more attractive "classroom" look.

2. If your room is unbearable with *NO HOPE OF IMPROVEMENT, SEE YOUR PRINCIPAL* about a change of location. Principals can be your greatest allies. They were teachers once, too!

3. If you've done all you can and it's still not right, wear a smile and let your students know you are willing to overcome a less than perfect classroom in order to be with them. They'll love you for it and will try harder to overcome *THEIR* problems.

3. AN ADULT IS NOT A CHILD
(NO KIDDING!)

If you have spent your teaching career surrounded by "little people", or for that matter anyone who comes in under the age of consent, chances are you have some habits which are pretty well entrenched. You are going to have to root them out and get rid of them.   Adult students are many things, but they are NOT CHILDREN. Do not treat them as such.

I remember one teacher (a longtime elementary school veteran) on her first evening in front of an adult class. Out of nervousness, apprehension, who knows what, she reverted to what she knew best...the 2nd grade. Hand on hip, frown on face, she tried to loom over her students...she's not all that big. It wasn't a huge success.

"We must remember," she intoned with carefully spaced syllables, "that our class begins at 6:00. It does not begin at 6:10 or 6:15. If you come in late you will be marked absent!"

So there!

A number of her students were not in attendance the next night ... nor ever again. They either decided school was as they had remembered it...terrible... and gave up the idea of class altogether, or they left to enroll in a different class. Let's hope they found one where they would be treated as adults. And ... ADULTS NEED RESPECT!

As a teacher of adults, you need to remember at all times that your students will *be there* (or NOT be there) because that is *their desire*. Do your job and present the information they wish to learn in a RESPECTFUL manner. Treat them as people worthy of the great gift of learning. Then they *will be there* and *on time* if it is at all humanly possible.

Most children are in school because they have no choice in the matter. Adults are there because they have needs and desires which makes education IMPORTANT for *them*.

RULE #3: RESPECT YOUR STUDENTS, OR YOU WON'T HAVE THEM!

4. DESIGN FOR SUCCESS!

Adult students come to you with many ingrained "school habits" and ideas of their own. Many of their thoughts and feelings about school will be negative. Even though the students are there of their own volition, it will take time for them to discover what a great, exciting and rewarding, thing education can be.

As teacher you can create a climate for your class. Make students comfortable, and let them know that you are there to help them meet their goals and aspirations.

Something as simple as a pot of coffee brewing in a corner of the room can help to put your students at ease. You can begin to allay their fears too by letting them see that you are tailoring their programs to suit their needs.

One of the best ways of doing this is to let the students *help* with the planning of their program. If they have a hand in the design of their course (with teacher guidance) they will have even more at stake in the outcome. The students too will be more aware than the teacher (who is meeting them for the first time) as to how they have best learned in the past.

That awareness must be coupled with what we know today of "learning styles" to help them best approach their education.   It is vital also to help them   realize the hard fact that they, AND THEY ALONE, are responsible for whether or not they learn. Be sure, however, to temper this "hard fact" with assurances that with their help you are going to design a program fitted to both their goals and their individual learning styles.

RULE #4: LET STUDENTS HELP DESIGN THEIR PROGRAM.

5. LEARNING WITH STYLE

Learning styles of adult students are as varied as the students themselves. Each student can be one style or a combination of several of the principal styles set forth by learning experts under the general heading of "Perceptual Learning Styles".

The basic learning styles are as follows:

1. PRINT: The student who learns best by reading the printed word is fortunate in that this and the "aural" are the two most frequently used avenues for teaching in our schools today. "Print" is, however, the least common of all adult learning styles!

2. AURAL: The learner who best retains that which he hears, like the "print" oriented learner, is in luck as the majority of teaching done today is still via the printed word and the lecture.

3. INTERACTIVE: The interactive learner likes to be "involved" with the learning process. This type of student is the "question asker", the one active in group discussions. "Give me participation! Give me exchanges!" (Resist the urge to say, "Give me a break!" This student's enthusiasm can sometimes spark the whole class).

4. TACTILE: The tactile learner needs to feel, handle, manipulate things. The use of "realia"* in the classroom is marvelous for this type. Nothing would be more frustrating for a tactile learner than signs which say "DO NOT TOUCH!"

5. VISUAL: The visual learner learns best by witnessing, seeing. Any kind of visuals...films, slides, videos, computer graphics make learning come alive.

6. KINESTHETIC: The kinesthetic learner seems to be always in motion. Often distracting in the classroom, this student is actually able to learn better while doodling, tapping a pencil, waving one foot, hopping up and down out of his seat and in general acting like a chimpanzee in overdrive. You might want to adapt your room for this

....

*Realia: real items used for demonstration in class...frequently used in ESL classes.

learner. Let the student have the opportunity to move around. Possibly let him have a spot isolated from others where his natural moving about will not disturb.

7. OLFACTORY: The person who is able to remember and learn best because of association of odors is the least common of all types of learners. (I have never figured out how the olfactory learner would master his multiplication tables, but possibly there's some connection between "nectarines and nines" or "oranges and eights, Chanel and the fives." Something like that!)

RULE 5. LEARN YOUR STUDENT"S OWN UNIQUE STYLE, AND USE   IT TO ITS BEST ADVANTAGE!

6. MAKING THE MOST OF YOUR APPROACH SHOT!

Before designing a particular student's program, let's concentrate on how to approach a classroom full of adults that first day or night. They may look like a mixed lot. They probably are as mixed as you can get. DO NOT PANIC! Your students probably have enough fear and panic to go around. Add any more and you may pop a transformer.

Remember Mary Anne .... smile a lot. Look your class over in a warm friendly, way that says, "Hey, I'm a nice person. This is going to be FUN!"

Let's say that you're going to be teaching an ABE/GED class. That probably means you will have a few young students (16-26 years of age) who dropped out of school for one reason or   another but who only need some intensive review before taking their GED test and getting their diplomas.

Then there will be the ones who dropped out of school in 7th or 8th grade years ago and have now decided to complete their education. They have forgotten their "book learning," but at ages 40 to 80 plus, although their sense of self-worth is fragile at best (due to lack of that high school diploma), they have picked up an immense amount of knowledge simply through the course of living.

An adult director in Florida speaks of how she has never met a student between the ages of 18 to 80 who did not have expertise in SOME area (carpentry, fishing, gardening etc.) that she, with her many degrees, does NOT have.

It is vital that you emphasize the vast amount of "pick-up" learning that your students have acquired. Let them know how important *you* think it is. Help make them aware of their hard won knowledge, and its value.

RULE #6:   EMPHASIZE YOUR STUDENT'S LIFE LEARNED KNOWLEDGE!

In with this "mixed bag" of students, you are going to have some plain, un-varnished illiterates (since we're speaking of ABE/GED) who have decided it was time to learn to read. The illiterates must be handled with great amounts of love and understanding. They may have been badly hurt along the way, and much of the hurt has been inflicted (hopefully non-intentionally) by well-meaning but over-worked teachers.

In the days before understanding of learning disorders, many teachers simply pushed the learning disabled to the back of the room and hoped that they wouldn't make too much   trouble. Now, here they are in   your room, together with the five high school kids who need a little brush-up ...and the three housewives who always meant to finish their education, but didn't. You've got your hands full!

It's a challenge and can be scary. The first class is a great time to break down barriers and put the students and yourself at ease.   (In our class a coffee maker is constantly brewing, the aroma itself making the   room more com- forting, more inviting, less threatening.)

If it is a class that is going to be taught group fashion (à la E.S.L or creative writing), you might have your students' desks or tables and chairs set in a semi-circle or circle. This way everyone will be able to see each other easily. Then you might want to give each student a folded card on which to print his name. It's a great way for the students to become familiar with one another.

In our imaginary ABE/GED mixed bag class we are going to be working individually with the students so the semi-circle does not work as well.

The first evening in a group class, time can be spent getting acquainted. In the mixed ABE/GED class, however, you will have students who do not want to stand up or speak out in a strange group. The last thing they want to do is to admit that they've never gotten their diploma, or that, worse yet, they can't read or write. It is important for you, the teacher, to get to know your students, but don't put them on the spot in front of their classmates.

RULE #7: BE SENSITIVE TO YOUR STUDENTS' FEELINGS.

So many adult learners are TERRIFIED of school failure. They have known so much of it in the past. Some of these dropouts left their failure in school and went on to lead very productive, successful lives, but when they re-enter the class-room, they feel the mantle of failure dropping over them again.

One of my favorite students was this type. He had dropped out of school in the eighth grade (he had only gotten that far by being "pushed" along. I'm certain he suffered undiagnosed dyslexia to a degree).

When I first met Harry, he was the well dressed president of one of the top rated businesses in the State of Florida. Clever and articulate, an avid tennis player, none of Harry's friends or associates knew that he had never gotten his high school diploma (let alone graduated from college!)

He came into my class, a 45 year old man who could have bought me and my husband many times over, and he became a fearful individual unsure of his self-worth and certain that he would NEVER BE ABLE TO LEARN ANYTHING! EVER! He was also very fearful of being seen in school by friends of his children or associates. While he was in class, we made a habit of closing the window blinds so no one could see in.

Harry gradually, with encouragement, began to find successes in class. He began literally to stop having nightmares about school and to discover that he not only *could* learn, but could learn very well. What surprised him the most was that he LIKED LEARNING!

Harry passed his GED after about four months of hard work and is now in college working towards his degree. He has no doubts whatsoever about his ability to achieve it. Neither do I.

RULE 8: MAKE YOURSELF AWARE OF YOUR STUDENTS' INDIVIDUAL HOPES AND DREAMS ... (ALSO THEIR FEARS AND SECRET TERRORS ABOUT EDUCATION!)

7. LET'S GET GOING!

When new students come in our ABE/GED class, we get them busy right away filling in forms, (a necessary evil). Although they have said they want to come to class to "get their GED", we watch closely to see whether their level is so low that they need help just filling out the registration form.

After they register, we give them a brief "Entry Survey" which we assure them is NOT A TEST! READ MY LIPS! NOT A TEST! We show each student (fleetingly) the answer key which we use to make individual prescriptions based on their specific needs.

Later, while we are checking over their Entry Surveys, we give them some type of interesting DIFFERENT work...different from any they might have remembered from their nightmares of school. (There are now many excellent materials designed particularly for the adult learner. Check in the appendix for addresses of major adult education publishers. They'll be more than happy to supply you with cataloges and often examination copies of materials.) If you have access to a computer, that can be a great ego booster for the fragile learner.

After we have checked to see what they need to work on, we have small, individual conferences with the students to let them know where they stand academically and what we think we can do to help them. MOST IMPORTANT...we find out about *EACH STUDENT*...what their goals are, their dreams, their hopes. What their backgrounds were in school. Why they dropped out. What their feelings are about it. Then we try to assure them that this class is somehow going to be different...that they can cash in on some of the vast experience that they have acquired in the two years? Ten years? Thirty years? Or how-ever long it has been since they have been out in the real world. This is the opportunity to assure them that they have not been operating in a vacumn but have been learning all along the way.

RULE 9: START YOUR STUDENTS WITH DIFFERENT, ADULT MATERIALS THAT RELATE TO THEIR SPECIAL INTERESTS.

8. CANDY, FLOWERS...
AND PICKLED OCTOPUS!

The adult learner brings many things to class with him: experience, maturity and a sincere desire to learn. Sometimes they also bring little tokens of their esteem. Flowers from a student's garden brighten the desk. Candies that span the spectrum from medicated cough drops and breath mints (am I coughing?...do I have cat's breath?) to handmade chocolate-dipped confections brighten the teacher's heart (and fatten her mid-section.) But unless you want to waddle your life away, it's a good idea to try to discourage little "gifties". Some students are hard to discourage. I have had all kinds of things brought in to class for me to sample and enjoy. Pickled octopus was not among my favorites.

A dear, little, Greek lady in our GED class kept promising to bring my team teacher and me her special "pickled you-know-what". We tried to convince her that we were not big on octopus, but she heard us not.

"You will LOVE this!" She assured us.

Three times she promised to bring it. Three times she accidentally left it home. She was distraught!   We were not.

The day she *remembered* to bring the octopus was a day when my team-teacher was off at a meeting. I was the lucky recipient of ALL of it.

I may some day speak with my partner again.

RULE #10: TRY TO DISCOURAGE GIFTS! GOOD LUCK!

9. SOME TYPES OF ADULT LEARNERS

Adult learners bring much more with them to class than yummies for the teacher. They bring along huge hampers full of pre-conceived notions about school and what it can and cannot do for them. They also bring along their abilities, experiences and handicaps. Let's look at different types of learners.

1. THE OLDER ADULT: Recent research shows that you can not only teach "old dogs" new tricks, but that they probably will come up with improvisations and improvements based on the "know-how" gained through long living.

These older adults may have some physical problems: poor eyesight, limited hearing ability etc., but often they have learned to adapt to their problems and compensate WELL in ways of which their younger counterparts would not have dreamed.

Your older students, once they have made the decision to come back to school, are usually extremely persistent in reaching their goals. I remember Odile, an 84 year old French lady in one of my E.S.L classes. She had been in this country for thirty years and had never needed to learn English until her son and husband were killed in an accident.

Odile had a hearing problem and suffered from high blood pressure. She did not drive and lived a long distance from the school in an area where bus service was poor. Yet she got up early every morning to catch the 6:30 bus which took her to the center of the city. From there she walked five long blocks to the adult center.

Our class was on the third floor. Sometimes the elevator worked. Often it did not. When it was recalcitrant, Odile would trudge her way up the three flights of stairs. She would be there every morning in her seat in the front of the room where she could see and hear best.

On days when it thundered and lighteninged, many of the young students (who drove cars to school) would stay at home Yet Odile would be there, via bus and shanks mare, in her pink plastic raincoat complete with matching umbrella .... a brave lady who made cowards of us all.

2. IMMIGRANT ADULTS: Immigrants and refugees have played a big part in the growth of the adult education field. The majority of them will be studying in E.S.L programs, but many who have a degree of proficiency with the English language show up in other classes for a variety of reasons.

Many who can communicate well verbally lack English reading and writing skills. The difference in alphabets is a hard stumbling block for them.

The fact that those from communist countries had to leave their records behind in the country from which they fled means even well-educated students must start over to get new credentials in this their adopted land. If you are fortunate enough to be assigned to an ESL class, get ready for the time of your life! Approaching your own comfortable, native language as someone else's "exotic foreign tongue" is a unique experience. You simply do not normally think of all the intricacies there are in this marvelous English language of ours, but teaching foreign students you MUST think about it constantly. The "whys" never stop coming. And they are so intriguing! For example: why is it that in English "slow down" and "slow up" mean the same thing when "up" and "down" are opposites? It is such fun!

You can hardly turn around in an E.S.L. class without it being a learning experience. I remember a teacher who dropped a piece of chalk and said, "Whoops!"

"Please, what ees theese 'whoops', Miss Patsy," her students asked.

It led to an interesting discussion on exclamations.

3. HANDICAPPED ADULTS: Adult education offers many programs for handicapped students over the age of 21. These classes range from basic life skills instruction to classes in home economics and adult basic education.

When teaching handicapped adults, particularly the mentally retarded, it is *vital* that you remember that you are dealing with ADULTS. Since many of their actions and reactions are childlike, it is all too easy to slip into the habit of treating them as children WHICH THEY ARE NOT!

Sally, a teacher who had worked for years with the adult mentally handicapped, tells of one time when the facility where she worked had to do extensive testing of students for an inventory of their skills and abilities.   At the end of two days of constant testing, both teachers and students were tired and irritable.

One of the more advanced, educable, retarded adults, Charles, had been through countless tests   many of which seemed childish and absurd to him. He was grouchy, and so was Sally. She had to test Charles for his ability to go into a fast food store and open a hamburger container. Since she was testing in the home economics room, Sally's hamburger container happened to be near a pile of sorted laundry (a different test). When Charles came in, Sally suggested (too abruptly she admits) that in the empty hamburger box was a nice, big, juicy hamburger with pickle and relish.

Charles gave Sally a look of disgust that said: "Who do you think you're kidding?" Then with one quick motion, he opened the empty box, put a rolled up sock from the laundry pile in it, closed the box and pushed it toward Sally.

"Here's your nice, big, juicy hamburger with pickle and relish, " He wrinkled his nose then gave a parting shot before going out the door: "Enjoy it…and have a nice day!"

4. "DISPLACED" HOMEMAKERS: These women are frequently among the most emotionally fragile students you will ever meet. Newly widowed or divorced, they often have just come through traumatic, emotionally devastating experiences and find themselves with children to support and no marketable job skills or education.   Adult education offers classes geared to these women's needs. They can get their high school diplomas then go on to learn a myriad of potentially lucrative skills. Your class can be an essential link to their future.   One memorable student had dropped out of school at 16, married at 17 and by age 25 was the mother of four children. When I first met her she was a newly divorced 30 year old with the self-image of a squashed cockroach. Beneath her disheveled, despondent exterior was a good, solid intelligence which came alive with a little encouragement and surprised her as much as anyone else. She obtained her GED in what had to be record time, but that was just the beginning!

While in school she had worked part time as a waitress and become interested in the restaurant business. When she received her GED, she went on to the local junior college. There she took restaurant management getting straight A's. Today she is managing a large seafood restaurant, and has recently been made a partner in the operation.

5. INSTITUTIONALIZED ADULTS: Many adult classes are offered within the correctional institutions of this country

as well as within both medical and mental hospitals. Tutors and basic ABE/GED classes help prepare the student for adjustment to life outside the institution.

In a letter from prison, an inmate wrote:

"I guss you no how herd haedit " (here there is an arrow pointing to a drawn face complete with "hard head") "I am Iv did it my way I didint lissan to pepol so my way got me back in prinson. This is the last time I'm chaching my ways I did test all week loing thay have G.E.D. 1 2 3 4 and I'm in 1 I'm working in a book called Laubach way to Reading Skill Book 3." (sic)

This letter was "written" in scrawly, difficult to read manuscript.

One month later, he wrote again, but this time in neat, readable cursive:

"I am still going to class. I got out of the Laubach Way to Read Book. Now I am in a English Book. I don't like English but I do it."

The letter had few mispellings in it, and the inmate was able to express his feelings in a clear manner. He may still have problems when he is released from prison, but his chances for permanent change are much enhanced by the improvement of his skills and the resultant improvement in his sense of self esteem.

6. ADULTS IN RURAL AREAS: People living in isolated sections sometimes need special programs to help them. Life on a farm ten miles from the nearest neighbor is a far cry from life in the city. Materials geared to their particular type of life need to be secured. Scour the publishers' catalogues * for books that will be pertinent and relative. In these rural areas too, home based instruction and one to one tutorial can be of great help.

7. ADULTS IN URBAN SITES: Students who live in high density, ethnic areas of high unemployment present a special problem to the teacher of adult education.

It takes great skill to motivate students who all too often come from homes where little emphasis has been placed on education. How can we impart the importance of education in an area where there is a high crime rate, and the students have seen that crime can appear to pay…and pay well? Not easily!

AGAIN…discover their goals, and pattern each particular program toward those goals. Give LOTS of feedback to the student on his progress.

Adolfo, a very bright Mexican student, had never had

....

* See list of major adult ed publishers in appendix

any education before he came to class. However, he had learned (street) English on his own, and had taught himself to read in both English and Spanish. (No mean feat). He'd also spent time in prison:

"Like man, I done it all. Ya know what I mean?"

I wasn't exactly sure and wasn't positive I wanted to know.

"Drugs, drinkin', life in the fast lane. I was a 'bad boy'," Adolfo informed me.

But underneath a tough facade was a gentle, pleasant person.

When we encountered him, Adolfo was employed as a bus boy in a Tex-Mex restaurant. His stated objective in coming to class was to learn to write and to do math. His goal was to become a waiter. (He also wanted to be able to write letters to his family.)

Adolfo adjusted his work schedule around his schooling because:

"That's the most important thing, man, ya know what I mean?"

I knew what he meant.

Adolfo's drive was great. The first week in class he spent laboring on his alphabet both manuscript and cursive. The beginning of the second week he copied a letter to his mother that he had dictated to a Spanish speaking teacher.

The third week he wrote a letter (in English) on his own to his younger sister in California (a treatise on the importance of education and how she should stay in school and work hard. (He wrote in English so that she would have practice in that language!)

Adolfo's writing and math are advancing rapidly. I'd love to see him become a doctor or lawyer. He probably could, but HE wants to become a waiter. We're helping him towards that goal. We are helping him with *his* life, not leading it ourselves.

8. ADULTS IN NURSING HOMES: Classes for the elderly or infirm can be challenging and particularly rewarding. Classes run the gamut from ABE/GED to exercises, arts and crafts, creative writing and many others. Many are the stories of withdrawn, almost catatonic, elderly people who, after weeks of "attending" simple classes suddenly speak for the first time in weeks or months or begin using their limbs or simply start responding to people.

One seldom knows what to expect when holding a class made up of the elderly. One teacher tells of a "poetry" class he held in a nursing home. He would read poetry and verse to the "students" and discuss it with them. He even had some of them reciting poems they remembered from their youth. He loved it. He thought they loved it too. I'm sure most of them did ... MOST of the time. But he tells of the day when he was reading poetry and the elderly students seemed completely wrapped up in the rythmic sound of the of the beautiful verses. They seemed mesmerized.

"I felt I had them in the palm of my   hand,"   he says. "It was wonderful!

"Then," he goes on, "I felt someone tapping my arm. I looked down and there was this little man in a wheel chair. The man looked up at me and asked, 'Do you have any cookies?' When I said, 'No,' this old guy frowned and asked:

'Then what in the H--- are you doing here?' "

Teaching can be a humbling experience.

RULE 11: ADULT LEARNERS COME IN MANY VARIETIES. BE READY FOR ANYTHING! (IF ASSIGNED TO A NURSING HOME, BRING STURDY EGO   AND COOKIES!*)

(*Never bring treats to a nursing home without checking with home director.)

10. THOSE *LOVELY* VOLUNTEERS...God Bless them!

Thanks largely to the media, there has been a growing awareness in the general population of the educational needs of our adults. This has resulted in a large number of volunteers appearing on the doorsteps of education seeking to help.

IF YOU ARE A TUTOR READING THIS, know that I think volunteers can be WONDERFUL! Our class could hardly exist without the assistance of the volunteers who give of their time and energy. Several of them are retired school teachers whose help is immeasureable particularly working with the illiterate members of our class who need so very much attention.

Care must be taken in the screening of volunteers, however, to make certain they are not going to be detrimental to the program. Once in, it can be awkward at best trying to oust an unpaid person particularly the individual who believes he or she is doing "something noble".

Amy, a teacher I know, had one memorable volunteer, a grandmotherly sort, "Madame X", who came regularly to class twice a week and nearly distroyed it before Amy eased her out.

Madame X's approach to the students was uniform:

"You mean you can't do that simple little problem? Why ANYONE can do that! Let me show you. I can do that BLINDFOLDED! Anybody could!"

Long after Amy had divested herself of Madame X, one of her students told how he had bumped into the erstwhile volunteer on the street. The student, one of Amy's favorite success stories, had come into class at age 62 a non-reader/writer. He could sign his name and that was all. After a year of work he had pulled himself up to reading on a fifth grade level and was writing letters to his family. (The first letter he wrote caused some consternation...his family had not known of his problem, but were so surprised to hear from him they called to see if anything were wrong.) When the student met Madame X on the street, the volunteer asked how he was doing. The student recounted his progress with understandable pride. Madame X responded as only she could:

"You know, before I met you, I didn't realize that ANYONE could ever live as long as 62 years without reading or writing!"

She *didn't* add, "you dumb idiot," but she might as well have.

Amy's student laughed it off and went on. He is now studying pre-GED Science and Social Studies and having a grand time.

Beside the volunteer who wants to come in and be "better than anyone else" in the class, there is the volunteer who wants a day out away from the wife or husband. They are not as harmful as the Madame X's of this world, but they must be guided a great deal to make sure they don't waste your students' time. Students frequently come to class at a tremendous expense of time and effort. They don't need that squandered.

We had one 83 year old "volunteer" who used to come in and "visit" with our students. I had to be constantly on the alert to see that he had enough productive things to do, or he'd visit the students to death. He especially liked to visit with one 66 year old gentleman, whom our elderly volunteer referred to as "That nice boy!"

If you are careful, (and fortunate) in the selection of the volunteers to work in your class you will find a large burden taken off your shoulders. A well trained and directed volunteer can work effectively with students, following along with student prescriptions (if you use a prescriptive system). They also can serve as wonderful speech models in ESL classes. Sometimes you will discover a volunteer whose strengths fit in well with a particular weakness of yours as a teacher (AND WE ALL HAVE THEM!!!)

My weakness is math. I can do it, but I will never be overfond of it. I have a wonderful volunteer, a retired auditor, who makes mathematical life blissful three times a week ·for my students. (Cheers my days a bit too!)

Things to remember about having volunteers is that you must train them carefully, patiently AND monitor them constantly. These two components are as important as screening. Remember too that these wonderful people are giving of their time to help you and your students. Their help can be invaluable. Show your appreciate heartily and OFTEN.

RULE 12:   IF YOU WANT HELP...SCREEN YOUR VOLUNTEERS CAREFULLY!   MAKE SURE THEY HAVE ADEQUATE TUTOR TRAINING!   AND REMEMBER TO SAY "THANK YOU, THANK YOU, THANK YOU!!!"

11. CHARACTERISTICS OF THE ADULT LEARNER

Aｄｕｌｔ LEARNERS FREQUENTLY:

1. FEEL INSECURE: Lack of self-confidence shows itself in many ways. These students are easily embarrassed and frequently perceive themselves as "dumb". They may deeply feel that "school is only for children". They can be easily hurt by a casual remark from anyone...teacher or volunteer. (Remember "Madame X"!)

2. HUNGER FOR SUCCESS: It has been a difficult decision to come back to school. Adult learners probably have so many memories of failure that if they do not achieve some kind of success (and quickly) they are very apt to give it up. It is up to you to see that they have immediate and positive feedback and encouragement. Success breeds success.

3. ARE STRONGLY MOTIVATED: They come to class with definite goals. Learn what they are. Plan their

program around them. You can help them meet their goals.

4. ARE SELF-DIRECTED: Malcomb Knowles defines self-directed learning as "a process in which individuals take the initiative, with or without the help of others, in diagnosing their needs, formulating learning goals, identifying human and material resources for learning, choosing and implementing appropriate learning strategies and evaluating learning outcomes." Your students will do their part. Do yours.

5. HAVE RESPONSIBILITIES: They have families, jobs or other claims on their time. Let them know that you are aware of this and will help them work around these other considerations in meeting their goals.

6. ARE FATIGUED: Due to responsibilities, work, family etc., adult students often come to class very tired. Any teaching technique which stimulates and wakes students up is helpful. (Don't forget the coffee!) Humor too is marvelous, but you don't have to be a Bob Hope. Just be upbeat and cheerful. It will go a long way towards making your adult students' burdens lighter.

7. ARE EXPERIENCED: Adult students' learning will be greatly influenced by their perceptions and reactions to past experiences. Learn about them. Build on their solid base of existing knowledge whatever it may be.

8. ARE UNIQUE: Like snowflakes, no two adult learners are the same. Each one must be approached as an individual....AND WITH GREAT CARE! EVER WATCH A SNOWFLAKE DISINTEGRATE?

<u>RULES TO REMEMBER</u>

1. WHEN WORKING WITH ADULTS, *ASSUME NOTHING!*

2. BRIGHTEN THE CORNER WHERE YOU ARE (EVEN IF IT'S A BUSY INTER-SECTION).

3. RESPECT YOUR STUDENTS, OR YOU WON'T HAVE THEM!

4. LET YOUR STUDENTS HELP DESIGN THEIR PROGRAM.

5. DISCOVER EACH STUDENT'S UNIQUE LEARNING STYLE AND USE IT TO ITS BEST ADVANTAGE.

6. EMPHASIZE YOUR STUDENTS' LIFE LEARNED KNOWLEDGE.

7. BE SENSITIVE TO YOUR STUDENTS' FEELINGS!

8. MAKE YOURSELF AWARE OF YOUR STUDENTS' INDIVIDUAL HOPES AND DREAMS...(ALSO THEIR FEARS AND SECRET TERRORS ABOUT EDUCATION).

9. START YOUR STUDENTS WITH *DIFFERENT* ADULT MATERIALS THAT RELATE TO THEIR SPECIAL INTERESTS.

10. TRY TO DISCOURAGE GIFTS...GOOD LUCK!

11. ADULT LEARNERS COME IN MANY VARIETIES. BE READY FOR ANYTHING! (IF ASSIGNED TO A NURSING HOME BRING STURDY EGO...AND COOKIES!)

12. IF YOU WANT HELP...SCREEN YOUR VOLUNTEERS CAREFULLY. MAKE SURE THEY HAVE ADEQUATE TUTOR TRAINING!

12. NOW ... FORWARD!

 Life in the adult education world is today, in many places, much improved over the dreary days of the 60's and early 70's when we were truly the "step-children" of the educational system.   Many of you today are almost "Cinderellas at the ball" in comparison. You will be able to step into new classrooms complete with training, materials, and...who knows...even a CHALKBOARD!   But the challenge is still there..challenge to meet the adult student on whatever level he happens to be and to help him achieve a richer, fuller life by attaining his goals.

It is a thrilling opportunity and one that cannot be measured by hours spent nor monies received. I wish you well in it. It's a great career and a tremendous challenge! But remember...you're working with adults now...NO KIDDING!

APPENDIX

PUBLISHERS OF ADULT MATERIAL*

BARNELL LOFT, LTD.
958 Church Street
Baldwin, New York 11510
(800) 645-6505

CONTEMPORARY BOOKS, Inc.
Wendy Harris
Department F89
180 North Michigan Ave.
Chicago, Illinois 60601
(800) 621-1918

CURRICULUM ASSOCIATES
5 Esquire Road
North Billerica, MA 01862-2589
(800) 225-0248

DELMAR PUBLISHERS INC.
Two Computer Drive, West
Box 15-105 - Albany, N.Y. 12212

EDL
P.O. Box 210726
Columbia, S.C. 29221
(800) 772-4035

EDUCATIONAL RESOURCES
2360 Hassell Road
Hoffman Estates, IL 60195
(800) 624-2926

FEARON EDUCATION
500 Harbor Boulevard
Belmont, California 94002
(800) 877-4283

JANUS BOOKS
2501 Industrial Parkway West
Dept KJA89
Hayward, CA 94545
(800) 227-2375

NEW READERS PRESS
Division of Laubach Literacy International
Department 98
Box 131
Syracuse, N.Y. 13210
(800) 448-8878

PHOENIX LEARNING RESOURCES
468 Park Ave. S.
New York , N.Y. 10016
(800) 221-1274

PRENTICE HALL REGENTS
CAMBRIDGE ADULT EDUCATION
Route 9W (Sylvan Avenue)
Englewood Cliffs, N.J. 07632
(800) 922-0579 or
(800) 225-7162

OXFORD UNIVERSITY PRESS
200 Madison Ave.
New York, N.Y. 10016
(800) 451-7556

STECK-VAUGHN COMPANY
P.O. Box 26015
Austin, Texa 78755 (800-531-5015

*These are only a few of the many fine publishers of
Adult Educational materials. Go to meetings! Haunt
the exhibitors hall! Dig in! Have fun!

Jane Hallock Combs recently completed her 19th year of teaching in adult education. She began working with adults in Rochester, New York, but since 1971 has been working in Pinellas County, Florida.

A native of Dobbs Ferry, New York, Jane holds a BA degree in English from St. Lawrence University, Canton New York. Her advanced studies have been at The University of South Florida.

She has published short stories and articles in many national magazines and is the co-author of ENGLISH: YOUR SECOND LANGUAGE published by Steck-Vaughn Co. and the author of MYSTERIES published by Harcourt, Brace Jovanovich.